Language Arts

Biographies Across the Curriculum

Grades 4–6

by Debra Kay Logan

LINWORTH LEARNING

From the Minds of Teachers

Linworth Publishing, Inc.
Worthington, Ohio

Library of Congress Cataloging-in-Publication Data

Logan, Debra Kay, 1958-
    Language arts : biographies across the curriculum, grades 4-6 / by
Debra Kay Logan.
        p. cm. -- (Kathy Schrock's every day of the school year series)
    Includes index.
    ISBN 1-58683-092-9 (Paperback)
    1. Language arts (Elementary)--United States. 2. Biography as a literary form--Study and teaching
(Elementary)--United States. 3.Language arts--Correlation with content subjects--United States. I.
Title. II. Series.
    LB1576.L594 2003
    372.6--dc21

                                                                    2003011167

Editor: Cindy Barden
Design and Production: Good Neighbor Press, Inc., Grand Junction, Colorado 81503

Published by Linworth Publishing, Inc.
480 East Wilson Bridge Road, Suite L
Worthington, Ohio 43085

ISBN: 1-58683-092-9

5 4 3 2 1

Table of Contents

Introduction

Biographies and Teaching Across the Curriculum

Is it possible for just one person to make a difference?

Imagine what the United States might be if there were no General George Washington. How would our lives be different if there were no Rosa Parks? Jazz wouldn't be jazz without Scott Joplin.

Biographies are a valid, exciting vehicle for teaching across the curriculum. Knowing about individual contributions breathes life and relevancy into learning. In this book, your students will research fascinating biographies to study language arts.

Using Biographies to Teach Language Arts

■ Writing

Your students have just researched the lives of Americans who have made dramatic contributions to our country. Before your class now lies a wealth of writing opportunities, from letters to eulogies to debate speeches. Whether labeling objects for a "museum" display or writing the text for a Power Point presentation, writing takes on a real-world feel.

Students also learn that various types of writing are required for different projects. When students are writing books for "publication," for example, conventions like spelling and grammar are forefront. Powerful phrases, on the other hand, make for a much more interesting postcard. An awareness of audience and a feeling of ownership are increased as students adjust how they write to fit a purpose.

■ Reading

Reading and researching are fundamentally connected. When taking biographical notes, students are exposed to a myriad of informational texts: encyclopedias, biographies, textbooks, biographical dictionaries, magazine articles, websites, and more.

■ Listening and Speaking

Your students can use their biography notes for any number of presentations: a re-enactment of an event in someone's life, a speech, a skit where several researched characters appear—your imagination is the limit. Meanwhile, students are learning how to speak clearly and listen to each other.

Consider these benefits:

◆ Not only does a student learn about his or her particular project, but also their classmates' when they share their projects with the class.

◆ Biographies are easily structured to fit your lessons in any other unit, be it math, science, social studies, art, etc.

◆ Biographical research and projects can accommodate visual, audio, and kinetic learning styles, and nurture different areas of intelligence as defined by Howard Gardner in *Frames of Mind: The Theory of Multiple Intelligences/Tenth Anniversary Edition* (Basic Books, 1993).

With everything to gain, you can't afford not to use *Biographies Across the Curriculum* for your language arts class.

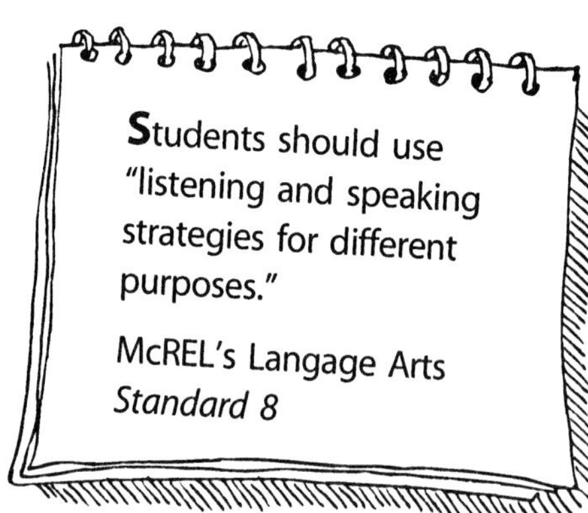

Try These Collective Biographies in Your Classroom

American Heroes of Exploration and Flight, Anne Schraff

American Dinosaur Hunters, Nathan Aaseng

Girls Think of Everything: Stories of Ingenious Inventions by Women, Houghton Mifflin

Lives of Musicians: The Good Times, the Bad Times (and What the Neighbors Thought), Kathleen Krull

Lives of Athletes: Thrills, Spills (and What the Neighbors Thought), Kathleen Krull

Oceanographers and Explorers of the Sea, Kirk Polking

Artists and Writers of the Harlem Renaissance, Wendy Hart Beckman

American Computer Pioneers, Mary Northrup

American Environmental Heroes, Phyllis Stanley

For a comprehensive look at how the units in this book meet the Mid-Continent Research for Education and Learning (McREL) Standards for Language Arts, see the included cross-reference chart. See the Curricular Connections Chart for how the units might connect with other subjects. For complete McREL details, see www.mcrel.org.

McREL Language Arts Standards addressed in units 1–5 of this book

McREL Standard	Unit 1 Basic Biography	Unit 2 Awesome Authors	Unit 3 Gods, Goddesses & Ancient Heros	Unit 4 Presenting Poets	Unit 5 Super Students & Terrific Teachers
1. Writing skills & processes	✓	✓	✓	✓	✓
2. Writing style & rhetoric		✓	✓	✓	✓
3. Writing grammar mechanics		✓	✓	✓	✓
4. Writing research	✓	✓	✓	✓	✓
5. Reading skills & strategies	✓	✓	✓	✓	✓
6. Reading literary texts		✓	✓	✓	
7. Reading information texts	✓	✓	✓	✓	
8. Speaking & Listening	✓	✓	✓	✓	
9. Viewing visual media	✓	✓			✓
10. Media characteristic & components	✓		✓		✓

In the McREL Language Arts Standards at levels II (Grade 3–5) and III (Grade 6–8), there are nearly 200 benchmarks. See www.mcrel.org for the complete standards list.

Curricular Connections Chart

Curricular Areas	Unit 1 Basic Biography	Unit 2 Awesome Authors	Unit 3 Gods, Goddesses & Ancient Heros	Unit 4 Presenting Poets	Unit 5 Super Students & Terrific Teachers
Language Arts	✓	✓	✓	✓	✓
Social Studies/History	✻	✓	✓		✓
Science	✻		✓		
Math	✻				
Technology	✓	✓	✓	✓	✓
Art	✻	✓	✓	✓	✓
Music	✻			✓	✻

✓ Indicates that the lesson has built-in connections.

✻ Indicates that it is possible to connect the lesson to the listed curricular area.

Using This Book

Each lesson in this book begins by having students create a biography as a springboard for a language arts activity. Unit-specific reproducibles are at the end of each unit, including a *Notetaking Sheet* for students, a *Self-Check Sheet* for students, and an *Assessment Rubric* for you. Reproducible sheets that can be used in more than one unit are in the Appendix, including *Biography Sign-Up Sheets*, where students can write their names next to their chosen person of study. See the Table of Contents for a complete list of resources available in the Appendix.

Each unit begins with suggestions for preparing your students and then follows with detailed instructions for teaching the unit. Teaching Tip boxes contain helpful hints for making lessons go smoothly. At the end of the book if you're ready for more, the Appendix contains a *Project Idea List* for extra biography activities.

Notetaking Sheets

A word about the *Notetaking Sheets*: They may appear to be worksheets, but they are not. Explain the difference to your students. Worksheets are expected to be totally filled out with complete sentences and are often the final project. A *Notetaking Sheet* may or may not be totally completed and should not have sentences *unless* the researcher is quoting a source. A *Notetaking Sheet* is a step in a process and never an end. It serves three important functions:

◆ To help the students pinpoint facts;

◆ To simplify selecting relevant information;

◆ To eliminate copying word-for-word from resources.

You do not always have to use the *Notetaking Sheets* provided in this book. Students—individually, in small groups, or as a class—can create them to ask their own essential questions.

Unit One

Basic Biography Skills

Overview

This lesson provides the basics for researching biographical information. Your students will use the *Mini Biographical Notetaking Sheet* to compile an Attaché File on their person of study. The Attaché File consists of *Faux Birth, Marriage, Award,* and *Death Certificates*. Students will learn about typical resources for biographical information with the *Biography Pathfinder Sheet* and how to credit those resources using the *Source Credit Sheet*. Students can use the *Biography Self-Check Sheet* to review their projects before handing in. Use the *Biography Rubric* to grade each project.

Time Required

Allow one class period.

Curriculum Connections

Across the curriculum. Use the *International Biography Sign-Up Sheet*, or the *American Biography Sign-Up Sheet* for a social studies connection. Or, use the blank *Biography Sign-Up Sheet* to create your own list of biographies to complement any subject your class may be studying.

Prerequisite Skills

Work with the librarian/media specialist to make sure that students have the needed Dewey, book attack, topic, and electronic search strategies and skills.

MATERIALS

All reproducibles are available at the end of this unit except the *Biography Pathfinder Sheet; the Source Credit Sheet; Image Credit Sheet; and the International, American,* or blank *Biography Sign-Up Sheets*, which are in the Appendix.

Students: *Mini Biography Notetaking Sheet, Faux Birth, Marriage, Death,* and *Award Certificates,* construction paper for attaché "case," *Biography Pathfinder Sheet, Source Credit Sheet, Image Credit Sheet* (if students download pictures for their projects), *Biography Self-Check Sheet,* computer workstations (with color printer), multimedia or LCD projector (optional), books, magazines, CD-ROM resources, and Internet access.

Teacher: *Biography Rubric* for each student, (see end of unit) and one of the following for each class (see Appendix).

◆ *International Biography Sign-Up Sheet,*

◆ *American Biography Sign-Up Sheet,* or

◆ *Biography Sign-Up Sheet* (use this to make your own list)

Preparing Your Students

Ask if your students know anyone famous. Does that make them more interested in what that famous person does? Learning about people makes their areas of study more exciting. Introduce several names from your *Biography Sign-Up Sheet*. If possible, link this biography project with current subjects your class is studying. For example, your class might be doing a unit on outer space. Have a list of well-known astronauts, astronomers, or scientists. If truly adventurous, dress up as one of the characters!

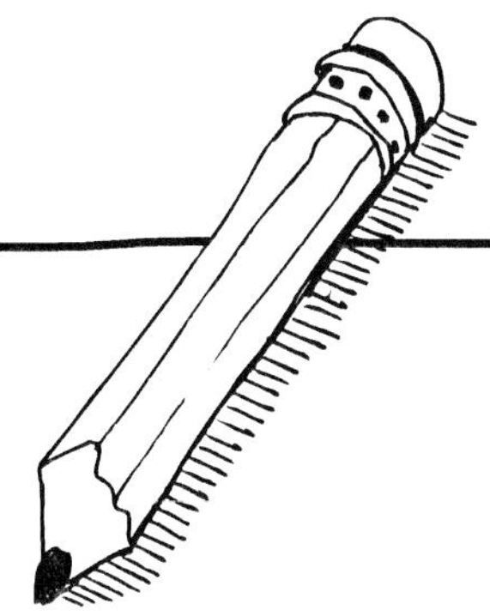

Ask students to think about which person they want to research as you explain the Attaché File. Distribute *Faux Birth*, *Marriage*, *Award*, and *Death Certificates* to each student, explaining what each one is. Will students need to use all of them for every character? Might students need more than one of any specific document?

If available, display past biography projects and involve students in assessing them. Talk about standards for assessment. Hand out or post copies of the *Biography Self-Check Sheet*. Finally, ask students to choose their persons to research, or assign them yourself, and fill out the *Biography Sign-Up Sheet* of your choice.

Introducing the Lesson

Distribute and review *Mini Biography Notetaking Sheet*, making clear that it is a notetaking sheet—not a worksheet (see How to Use This Book for a discussion of the differences). If you assigned persons to be researched, write the names and student names beforehand on the *Notetaking Sheets*. Explain how the *Notetaking Sheets* work:

■ Information should not be in complete sentences and should not be copied word for word from the source. Direct students to skim-read the sources for birth, death, and marriage dates and any awards won. Students should jot phrases in their own words.

■ **C**larify any new vocabulary.

◆ Use overhead or white/chalk board to show the ways that birth, marriage, and death dates are represented in reference works. For example:

Important Dates

(1823–1912)

b. 1823 *d.* 1912

m. 1840

(1947–)

b. 1823 (Marion, Ohio) *d.* 1912 (Paris, France)

c. 1823

◆ First post the dates in parenthesis and ask the group what it means.

◆ Then show the **b.**, **m.**, and **d.** abbreviations and ask what they represent.

◆ Introduce the "**m.**" abbreviation and ask students to guess what it means. At least one student will figure out what it represents.

◆ Finally, introduce "**circa**" and what it means. Ask students, "Over a hundred years ago would people have gotten a new calendar every year?" Then ask if people always would have known the day's date. Also talk about how records can be lost and destroyed (fire, flood, carelessness, etc.).

■ **H**elp students brainstorm what kind of information can be used to summarize a person's life. A good way to start the discussion is to ask students what kind of information they would use to summarize their own lives.

TEACHING TIP

Talk about missing death dates and what they mean. Remind students that they do not have to fill in all the blanks on *Notetaking Sheets*. Point out that it is not a good idea to "bury a living person" in order to fill in a blank! Also, suggest that if there is no death date, they should consider checking the date of their resource. If a source is more than two or three years old, students should verify dates in a newer resource.

Where to Research

- **H**aving discussed what information is needed and how it is to be used, the next step is to explore possible research resources. Distribute *Biography Pathfinder Sheet*. Begin by asking students if they think they will need extensive information or brief facts. When they say brief facts, ask them what type of resource would be best. They should say biography. Then ask how they would go about finding specific facts in a biography. With direction, they will figure out that an index or table of contents will be the best places to start.

- **A**sk students to predict other possible resources. As they mention different types of resources, talk about how each is used. Review things such as using quotation marks or hyphens when searching a name online. Remind students to look up biographical information using a person's last name in print resources. When discussing encyclopedias (print, CD-ROM, and online), say, "They are a great place to start if you do not know anything about the person you are researching."

- **W**hen students are through suggesting possible resources, highlight ones they may have missed. This is usually a great time to share biographical dictionaries and collective biographies. Remind students once they have identified their peoples' fields of endeavor, they can also search under topics relating to the appropriate fields.

- **D**iscussed resources should include biographical dictionaries, encyclopedias (print, CD-ROM, and online), biographies, Internet sites, collective biographies, and print and nonprint resources.

- **F**inally, have students use the *Biography Pathfinder* to plot out a research plan.

How to Credit Research Sources

Distribute the *Source Credit Sheet*, reminding students that they will need to credit any sources they use. Discuss how to fill it out. Demonstrate by making a transparency of the sheet and filling a couple of sample entries on the overhead.

■ **W**hile demonstrating, show how to find information like:

◆ publisher,

◆ place of publication,

◆ copyright date,

◆ author of encyclopedia articles,

◆ author of Web pages,

◆ URL (Web page address).

■ **I**f sound or movie files are apt to be available online for individuals being researched, use the multimedia or LCD projector to demonstrate how to copy, save, name, insert (into hypermedia projects), and play these multimedia files.

■ **I**f students have the opportunity to download images off the Internet or photocopy images from text, hand out *Image Source Sheet*. Use the same techniques as above to demonstrate how to fill out the sheet. If necessary, have a mini-lesson on how to download images or use the photocopier.

As Students Work

Assist students as they research. Watch for copying sources word-for-word and help individual students make the transition to taking notes. Remind students to look in multiple resources and not spend all their time in the encyclopedias!

Compiling the Project

◆ As students finish their research, direct them to begin work on their Attaché Files. Encourage students to use neat handwriting to make the attaché documents look as authentic as possible.

◆ They may not need all the documents, or they may need more than one of any specific document. For example, their character may have been married twice (two marriage certificates), and have won three awards (three award certificates).

◆ Fold a piece of construction paper in half to make an attaché "case" to store the documents.

Self-Check

Once their projects are nearing completion, remind students to look at the *Biography Self-Check Sheet* you handed to them at the beginning of the lesson. Have them assess their own work, or trade with a partner for gentle critique. Then, give students time to polish their projects.

Sharing With the Class

If you have time, ask students to share their Attaché Files and the information they have found with the rest of the class, either by breaking into small groups or by giving individual presentations. The Appendix contains a *Storytelling Tips Sheet* for presenters and a *Presentation Notes Sheet* on which listeners can record feedback

Adaptations and Extensions

■ **C**elebrate with an award ceremony! Ask each student to create an award appropriate to his/her researched person. Students will explain the awards and what the "winners" did to earn them. Have students make award certificates using a program like Print Shop or Print Master or use the *Faux Award Certificate* in the Appendix.

■ **C**reate a class slide show/multimedia presentation with a slide/card for each person. After presenting the slide/presentation show to the class, save it and display it during parent-teacher conferences, open houses, etc.

■ **U**se timeline software like *TimeLiner* to make a timeline of an individual's life or groups of individuals.

■ **S**tudents can use a program like Print Shop, PrintMaster, or Microsoft Publisher to create an illustrated sign with the person's name, life span, and a clipart symbol. Use a multimedia projector or LCD panel to demonstrate working with a desktop publishing program. Show:

◆ Creating a new sign type document.

◆ Adding text to the document.

◆ Changing text style and size.

◆ Selecting and adding graphics to a document.

◆ Saving a document.

■ **V**isit the *Project Idea List* in the *Appendix* of this book for additional extension ideas.

Reproducible

Name ________________________________

Biography Project

Name: ________________________________

Date of birth: ________________

Date of death:________________

Education (if any): ________________________________

____

Accomplishments (why famous): ________________________________

____

____

____

____

____

Awards (if any): ________________________________

Interesting facts: ________________________________

____

____

____

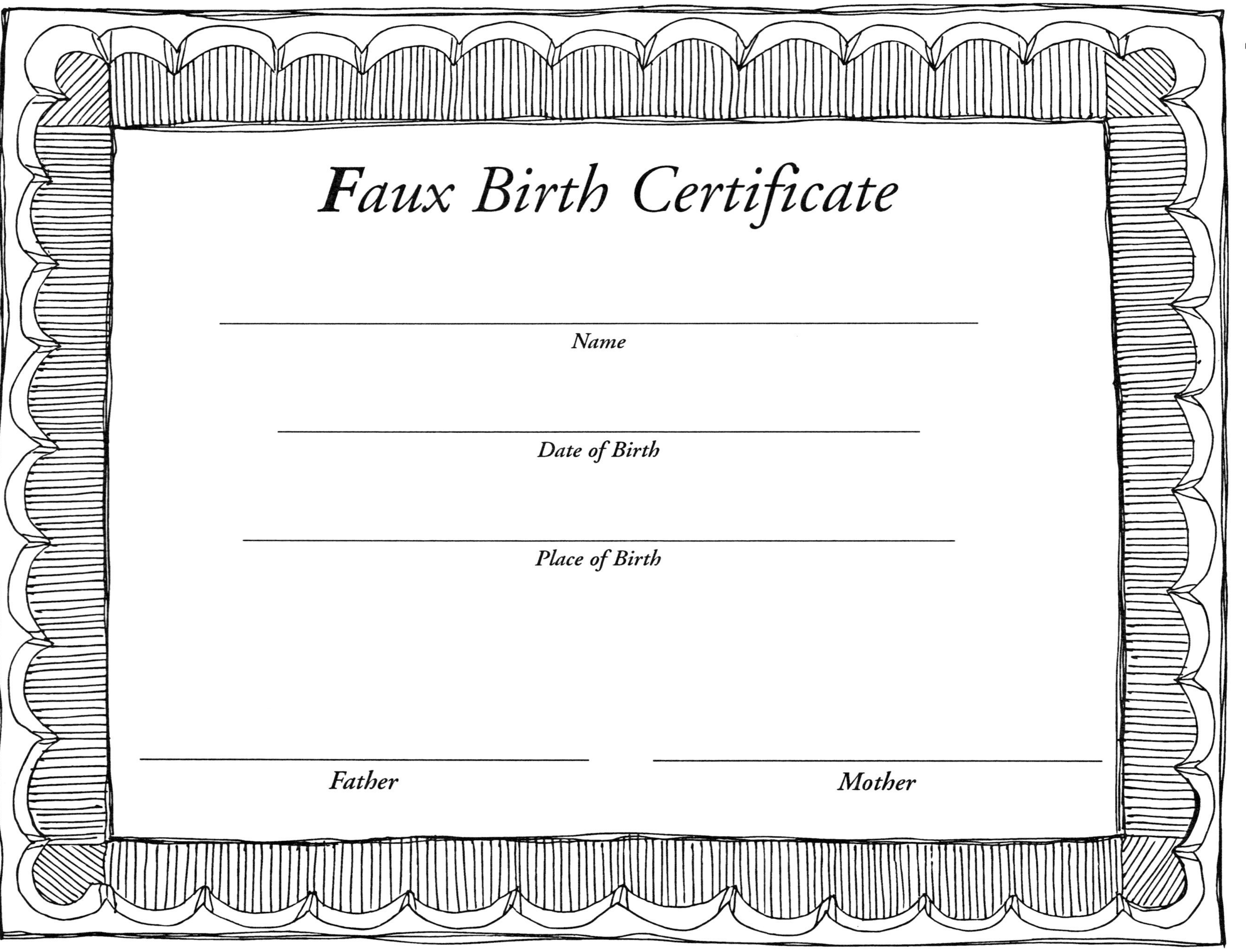
Faux Birth Certificate
Name
Date of Birth
Place of Birth
Father
Mother

Faux Marriage Certificate

On this date

and

were joined in HOLY MATRIMONY.

Reproducible

Faux Death Certificate

Name

Date of Death

Place of Death

Cause of Death

Faux Award Certificate
Name
Award(s)

Basic Biography Self-Check Sheet

Name _______________________________

Title/Project _______________________________

Check the word in each section that best describes your project.

	Not yet! ☹	Sometimes	Often	Yes! ☺
My project is full of information which is accurate, clear, complete, and detailed.				
I credited my sources.				
My writing is neat, easy to read, and makes sense.				
My punctuation, spelling, capitals, and grammar are correct.				
I labeled my work to help people understand my project. My labels explain my project and what I have learned.				
I followed directions.				
Project: My project was well planned. I chose a good way to show my information.				
Art Project: I used lots of color, and was neat and careful when I worked. My project is unique.				
Presentation Project: I was loud and easy to hear. I used visual aids well.				
Dramatic Project: I acted with feeling. I used costumes, scenery, and props. It was a good production.				
Writing: My writing is realistic and creative. I have great details.				

Comments on back:

Name _______________________ Date ____ / ____ / ____ Title/Project _______________________

Basic Biography Rubric

	Apprentice ☹	Journeyman	Master ☺		
	1	2	3	4	
Information: inaccurate, unclear, incomplete, lacking details, credit is not given when appropriate, evidence of copying					Accurate, clear, complete, detailed, sources credited, original work
Mechanics: sloppy, poor spelling, missing capitalization and/or punctuation, poor grammar, difficult to read, illogical, unorganized					Neat, careful, accurate spelling, correct capitalization and punctuation, good grammar, easy to read, logical, organized
Labels or Explanations: no labels or explanations					Labels or explanations help the "audience" to better understand the information presented
Project Basics: unrealistic, lacking details, does not communicate information, poor use of medium, poorly planned, did not follow directions					Realistic, good details, communicates information, good use of medium, evidence of planning, followed directions
Art Project: lacks color, not original, sloppy					Colorful, original, careful, neat
Presentation Project: hard to hear, poor planning, no or poor use of visuals					Loud and clear, well planned, used visual aids well
Dramatic Project: lacking drama, poor production (technical, costumes, sets, props, etc.)					Dramatic, good production (technical, costumes, sets, props, etc.)
Writing Project: inconsistent (see mechanics), unclear					Consistent (see mechanics), clear
	1	2	3	4	
	Apprentice ☹	Journeyman	Master ☺		

Comments on back:

Unit Two

Awesome Authors and Primary and Secondary Sources

Overview

Students use the *Awesome Author Notetaking Sheet* to gather biographical information about authors for one of the projects below. Students will also read *Primary and Secondary Sources* and fill out *What's Your Source? Sheet.* Students review typical research resources with the *Biography Pathfinder Sheet*, and use the *Source Credit Sheet* to credit those resources. Finally, students use the *Awesome Authors Self-Check Sheet* to review their projects. Use the *Awesome Authors Rubric* to grade each project.

Option 1: *Awesome Author Slide Show:* Using a hypermedia program like HyperStudio or Power Point, each student creates a series of slides featuring the picture of and information about their author. If students are inexperienced presentation software users, this can be a partner activity.

Option 2: *Awesome Author Trading Card and Book Review:* Students create an *Awesome Author Trading Card* highlighting important facts and best-known works of the author. They also write an *Awesome Author Book Review* about their favorite book by this author.

Time Required

Instruction and Research: Two class periods.

Compiling the Projects

> *Slide Show:* Introducing the presentation software and its capabilities should take half a class period. The time needed to create slides will depend on the availability of software and computer lab workstations.

> *Trading Card and Book Review:* One class period.

Presentations: Two class periods.

Curriculum Connections

Slide Show: Technology, art, literature, reading, writing, and speaking.

Trading Card and Book Review: Art, literature, reading, writing, and speaking.

Prerequisite Skills

Students should have some familiarity with their author's writings. Work with the librarian/media specialist to make sure that students have the needed Dewey, book attack, topic, and electronic search strategies and skills.

MATERIALS

All reproducibles for this lesson are available at the end of the unit except the *Biography Pathfinder Sheet, Source Credit Sheet, Image Credit Sheet,* and *Biography Sign-Up Sheet,* which are in the Appendix.

Students: *Awesome Authors Notetaking Sheet, Primary and Secondary Sources Sheet, What's Your Source? Sheet, Biography Pathfinder Sheet, Source Credit Sheet, Awesome Authors Self-Check Sheet, Source Credit Sheet, Image Credit Sheet* (if students download pictures for their projects), books, magazines, CD-ROM resources and Internet access, computer workstations (with color printer),

- ◆ *Slide Show:* Multimedia projector or LCD panel (if available), a presentation program such as HyperStudio or Power Point.

- ◆ *Trading Card and Book Review: Awesome Author Trading Card* and *Awesome Author Book Review*

Teacher: *Awesome Authors Rubric* for each student, and *Biography Sign-Up Sheet.*

Preparing Your Students

Ask students to think about a book they really enjoy. Ask for volunteers to tell briefly why they like a particular book. Has anyone had a chance to meet an author at a book signing? Discuss how knowing about who wrote a book can make the book more exciting. Explain that each student will choose an author to learn about.

◆ *Slide Show:* Show an example of a presentation program slide show or card stack. Tell students that they will gather information about an author for the same type of presentation. If students are to work with partners, ask them to choose a partner now.

◆ *Trading Card and Book Review:* Distribute and review *Awesome Authors Trading Card* and *Awesome Author Book Review.* If available, show past *Awesome Author* projects. Tell students that they will gather information about an author for the same project.

Introducing the Lesson

Distribute and review the *Awesome Authors Notetaking Sheet.* (See discussion on *Notetaking Sheets* in How to Use This Book.)

■ **R**emind students that authors are not all alike (i.e. not all have won awards). Have students predict which parts of the *Notetaking Sheet* might not fit all of the authors (i.e. awards, death dates, children, etc.).

■ **A**ssign or allow selection of author. If students have trouble choosing their own authors, ask them to consider authors of their favorite books. Fill out the *Biography Sign-Up Sheet* so you have a record of students' selections.

Primary and Secondary Mini-Lesson

Prepare Your Students

Ask students if some sources are more reliable than others. Share this scenario of firsthand knowledge versus secondhand knowledge.

> "The principal told me that we are going to have free ice cream for lunch and an extra recess tomorrow." (Firsthand)

> "One of the students told another student that he heard that we are going to have free ice cream for lunch and an extra recess tomorrow." (Secondhand)

Ask students which source of information is more likely to be reliable and why. Have them identify which source is a firsthand or primary source and which one is secondary.

Work As a Class

Distribute *Primary and Secondary Sources Sheet* and give students a few minutes to read it silently to themselves. If you prefer, choose readers to read aloud. Begin a class discussion:

- **W**hat is the difference between a primary and secondary source? What are some examples of primary sources? Secondary sources? Can some items be both?

- **L**et students work in small groups to brainstorm examples of primary and secondary sources. Discuss their findings as a class.

- **D**iscuss if primary sources are always reliable? Why or why not?

  - When two people see the exact same thing, do they always describe it in the exact same way? Talk about bias and point of view.

  - If two or more people try to figure out what the same thing means, do they always come up with the same answer?

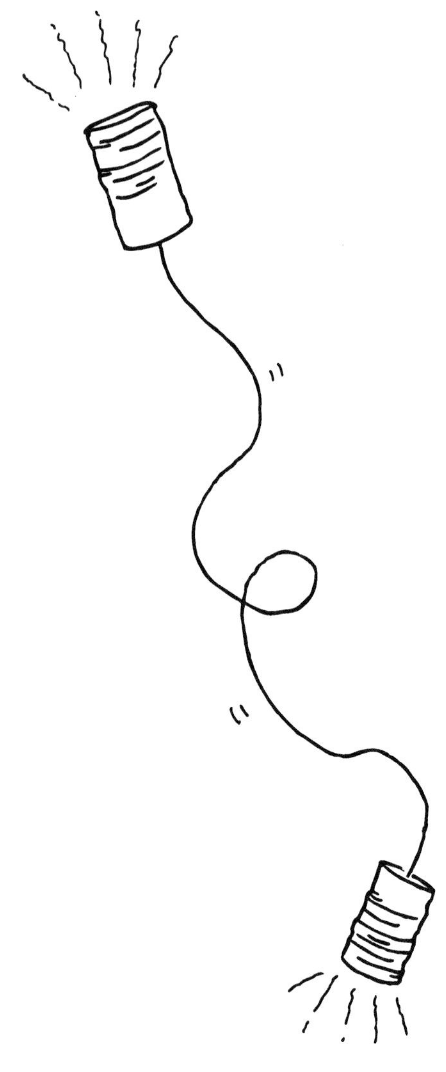

- ■ **W**hat questions can be asked to verify a primary source is reliable?

  - ◆ Who created the source?

  - ◆ Why was it created?

  - ◆ Is there any reason the creator would mislead others?

  - ◆ Who was the intended audience? Was the source to be private?

  - ◆ When was the source created? Immediately? Later?

- ■ **D**iscuss how they can use this information in their research.

- ■ **D**ivide students into small groups and distribute *What's Your Source? Sheet*. Give them fifteen minutes to work on them; then, discuss the answers as a class.

Where to Research

- ■ **D**istribute *Biography Pathfinder Sheet* and brainstorm resources with your students. This a great project for introducing specialized author resources, the Internet, online databases, encyclopedias, and other print resources.

- ■ **H**elp students to develop a research plan by having them think about which resources will be the best for getting started. Ask questions such as, "Do you want your fast facts or your details first?" and "Where are some of the places that may include a picture of your author?"

- ■ **R**emind students that book jackets can be sources for biographical information.

- ■ **E**ncourage them to think about the amount of information needed.

As Students Work

◆ Assist students as they research. Watch for copying sources word-for-word and help individual students make the transition to taking notes. Remind students to look in multiple resources and to credit their sources on the *Source Credit Sheet*.

◆ If students download pictures of their authors off the Internet, they will need to record the source of the image on an *Image Source Sheet*. If students need to save images to disks, remember to label each disk and keep a record of students' names and corresponding file names.

How to Use the Presentation Technology

On the second research day, break for a few moments to give the students a tour of what the presentation software can do and how to use it using the multimedia projector. Demonstrate:

1. Creating a new card/slide set.

2. Selecting or creating a background.

3. Inserting and formatting text.

4. Inserting graphics, sounds, tables, etc.

5. Pointing out how to navigate in the program.

6. How to save the work.

Discuss that slides will need to be legible. Have them suggest ways they can make their slides readable. Background and text should be discussed. Also the *Seven by Seven Rule* should be used. Slides should be limited to no more than seven lines and no more than seven words per line. Having fewer lines and words is great!

When students are ready to create their slides:

- **G**roups will need to decide what information will be shared on each slide/card to create a unified look for the project. Each card needs a home button and a link to the next card. Students get to select backgrounds, icons, sounds, font styles, objects, transitions, and animations.

Compiling the Project

As students finish their research, direct them to begin work on their projects. Remind them that spelling and grammar count!

- ◆ *Slide Show:* Give students time to practice their presentations, so they become comfortable with using the technology and speaking in front of the class.

- ◆ *Trading Card and Book Review:* Encourage neat handwriting. Remind students that they are trying to "sell" why they like this author and book.

Self-Check

Once their projects are nearing completion, refer students to the *Biography Self-Check Sheet* you handed to them at the beginning of the lesson. Have them assess their own work, or trade with a partner for gentle critique. Then, give students time to polish their projects.

Sharing With the Class

While the *Slide Show* lends itself to individual presentations, the *Trading Card and Book Review* project does not necessarily. If you have time, allow students to present individually. If not, break into groups.

The Appendix contains a *Storytelling Tips Sheet* for presenters and a *Presentation Notes Sheet* on which listeners can record feedback.

Adaptations and Extensions

- **H**ave students create their own essential questions about authors instead of using the *Awesome Authors Notetaking Sheet*.

- **R**equire students to select, read, and review a work by their authors. Post student *Awesome Authors Book Review Sheets* on the bulletin board.

- **H**ave the class create a map showing where in the world their authors live.

- **A**rrange a field trip to another classroom to share the students' presentations.

- **H**ave the authors "write" letters or postcards to each other. Assign or allow students to choose writing partners. Give them a brief meeting prior to starting the letter writing process. They will need to decide on possible topics for the letters and decide who will start first. This could evolve in to a mini research project on the times and places in which the authors live(d).

- **L**ook at book jackets and the biographical sketches of the authors. Have students write a biographical sketch of their author for a book jacket.

- **D**ecorate the room with homemade "dummy" covers of books by the *Amazing Authors*.

- **V**isit the *Project Idea List* in the *Appendix* of this book for additional extension ideas.

Awesome Authors Notetaking Sheet

Name ___________________________________

Author's Name ______________________________________

Date of birth: ___________________   Date of death: ___________________

Place of birth: ___________________

Background information:

Father: _______________________________   Mother: _______________________________

Siblings (brothers & sisters): ____

____

Spouse (husband or wife—if married): ____

Children: ____

____

Education (if any): ____

____

Place(s) lived: ____

____

Jobs: ____

____

____

Attach another sheet as needed.

Awesome Authors Notetaking Sheet

Personal stories (childhood, family, adult life, etc.): _______________________________

____

____

____

____

____

Did this author have any special writing training? _________

What kind of training? ____

____

What type of works (children's, poetry, plays, nonfiction, mysteries, etc.) does this author write?

____

____

List some of the author's famous works: _______________________________________

____

____

____

____

Attach another sheet as needed.

Awesome Authors Notetaking Sheet

Why is this author famous? What makes his/her writing special? _______________

____

____

____

____

What awards, if any, has this author won? ____________________________________

____

____

____

____

Share any other interesting facts about the author: ______________________________

____

____

____

____

____

____

____

Attach another sheet as needed.

Primary and Secondary Sources

Name _______________________________

What are primary sources?

Primary source materials are original items and records from the past. They can include documents like birth certificates, marriage licenses, journals, diaries, letters, and report cards. Primary source materials can be things like photos, maps, videos, film, cds, speeches, and interviews. Objects like clothing, weapons, and tools are also examples of primary source materials.

What are secondary sources?

Secondary sources are not original. Secondhand sources are created at a later time by people who were not at the event or place. A history book, news story, or a letter are examples of secondary sources.

Are primary source materials always accurate and the best sources of information?

◆ When two people see the exact same thing, do they always describe it in the exact same way?

◆ Do people always tell the truth?

◆ Do people sometimes want to influence other people?

◆ If two or more people try to figure out what the same thing means, do the people always come up with the same answer?

Since primary source materials may not always tell a whole or accurate story, it is a good idea to ask questions about primary source materials and to make decisions about which ones to use and how to use them. When looking at primary sources, ask yourself:

1. Who created the source?

2. Why was it created?

3. Is there any reason the creator would mislead others?

4. Who was the intended audience? Was the source to be private?

5. When was the source created? Immediately? Later?

Reproducible

Name _______________________________

Is it primary? Is it secondary? OR could it be either? Think about the types of sources listed and tell what kind of source each is and why.

1. **Newspaper**—Primary ______, secondary ______, or possibly both ______?

    Why?____

2. **Birth certificate**—Primary ______, secondary ______, or possibly both ______?

    Why?____

3. **Letter to a friend**—Primary ______, secondary ______, or possibly both ______?

    Why?____

4. **Diary**—Primary ______, secondary ______, or possibly both ______?

    Why?____

5. **Photo album**—Primary ______, secondary ______, or possibly both ______?

    Why?____

6. **History book**—Primary ______, secondary ______, or possibly both ______?

    Why?____

7. **Scrapbook**—Primary ______, secondary ______, or possibly both ______?

    Why?____

8. **Tombstone**—Primary ______, secondary ______, or possibly both ______?

    Why?____

Awesome Authors Trading Card

____
Author's Name

Top 5 Books!

- ◆ _______________________
- ◆ _______________________
- ◆ _______________________
- ◆ _______________________
- ◆ _______________________

Picture of author courtesy of

____

This author's writing is special because:

____
____
____
____
____
____
____

Interesting info:

____
____
____
____
____

❧ Just the Facts ❧

Birth date _______________________   Birth place _______________________

Education _______________________

Past Jobs _______________________

Family—spouse _______________________   children _______________________

Lives(d) in _______________________   Died _______________________

Reproducible

Name _______________________________

____
Student's name

Presents . . .

An Awesome Author Book Review

of

____
book title

A little bit about the story . . .

I recommend this story because . . .

Reproducible

Awesome Author Self-Check

Name _______________________________

Title/Project _______________________________

Check the word in each section that best describes your project.

	Not yet! ☹	Sometimes	Often	Yes! ☺
My project is full of information which is accurate, clear, complete, and detailed.				
I credited my sources.				
My writing makes sense. I have great details.				
My punctuation, spelling, capitals, and grammar are correct.				
I labeled my work to help people understand my project. My labels explain my project and what I have learned.				
I followed directions.				
Project: My project was well planned.				
Art Project: My backgrounds and text are pleasant to look at and easy to read. I used graphics to illustrate my information. My project is unique and has a consistent look.				
Presentation Project: I was loud and easy to hear.				
Dramatic Project: I acted with feeling. I used costumes, scenery, and props. It was a good production.				

Comments on back:

Name _____________ Date ___ / ___ / ___ Title/Project _____________

Awesome Author Project Rubric

	Apprentice ☹		Journeyman	Master ☺	
	1	2	3	4	
Information: inaccurate, unclear, incomplete, lacking details, credit is not given when appropriate, evidence of copying					Accurate, clear, complete, detailed, sources credited, original work
Mechanics: sloppy, poor spelling, missing capitalization and/or punctuation, poor grammar, difficult to read, illogical, unorganized					Neat, careful, accurate spelling, correct capitalization and punctuation, good grammar, easy to read, logical, organized
Labels or Explanations: no labels or explanations					Labels or explanations help the "audience" to better understand the information presented
Project Basics: unrealistic, lacking details, does not communicate information, poor use of medium, poorly planned, did not follow directions					Realistic, good details, communicates information, good use of medium, evidence of planning, followed directions
Art Project: backgrounds and texts are illegible, graphics illustrate information, has a unique and consistent look					Background and texts are readable, graphics illustrate information, has a unique and consistent look
Presentation Project: hard to hear, poor planning, no or poor use of visuals					Loud and clear, well planned, used visual aids well
	1	2	3	4	
	Apprentice ☹		Journeyman	Master ☺	

Comments on back:

Gods, Goddesses, and Ancient Heroes

Overview

Students will research a Greek or Roman god, goddess, or hero using *Gods, Goddesses, and Ancient Heroes Notetaking Sheet*. Students summarize a mythical story about their individual, polish their project with *Gods, Goddesses, & Ancient Heroes Self-Check Sheet*, and sketch their mythological being, share their summaries with the class. While listening to presentations, students fill out *Who's Who of the Gods and Goddesses* and use that information to fill out *It is All Greek Word Connections Sheet* and *Who Will Buy a Piece of the Past? Sheet*. Finally, use the *Gods, Goddesses, and Ancient Heroes Rubric* to grade each project.

Time Required

Instruction and Research: Two class periods.

Compiling the Project: One class period. Additional time may be required if students are to do their artwork during class time.

Presentations: Two class periods for student presentations and ½ class period for worksheets.

Curriculum Connections

Art, astronomy, literature, reading, writing, and speaking.

Prerequisite Skills

Students should have some background understanding of Ancient Greece and Rome, the role of mythology in their cultures, and a basic introduction to constellations and astronomy. If students need this information, review it in the Preparing Your Students section. Work with the librarian/media specialist to make sure that students have the needed Dewey, book attack, topic, and electronic search strategies and skills.

All reproducibles for this lesson are available at the end of the unit except the *Biography Pathfinder Sheet, Source Credit Sheet,* and *Image Credit Sheet,* which are in the Appendix.

Students: *Gods, Goddesses, and Ancient Heroes Notetaking Sheet; Gods, Goddesses, & Ancient Heroes Self-Check Sheet; Who's Who of the Gods and Goddesses Sheet; It is All Greek Word Connections Sheet; Who Will Buy a Piece of the Past? Sheet; Biography Pathfinder Sheet; Source Credit Sheet,* computer workstations, books, CD-ROM resources, and Internet access. Project materials: paper, markers, crayons, and/or colored pencils.

Teacher: *Gods, Goddesses, and Ancient Heroes Biography Sign-Up Sheet,* and *Gods, Goddesses, and Ancient Heroes Rubric* for each student.

Preparing Your Students

A good version of the Arachne story is William F. Russell's *Classic Myths to Read Aloud* (Crown, 1989). This anthology is also an approachable resource for student use as well.

Begin this lesson by telling a myth as a told story. Pick one that is not the only story associated with the god, goddess, or hero in the story. Ideally, it is good to choose one that has clear ties to our culture today. A good one is the story of Arachne. Students usually connect Arachne to arachnids without any prompting at the end of the story. The role myths played in ancient cultures should be covered at this time, unless it has been covered prior to the research session. Announce that students will be researching a god, goddess, or ancient hero and telling that myth to the class just as you did. Assign the characters, or have students choose for themselves. Fill out the *Gods, Goddesses, and Ancient Heroes Sign-Up Sheet.*

Introducing the Lesson

■ **D**istribute and review *Gods, Goddesses, and Ancient Heroes Notetaking Sheet* with students, reminding them that it is a notetaking sheet—not a worksheet (see How to Use this Book for a discussion of the differences). Establish why most mythological beings have both Greek and Roman names.

■ **A**sk students if having two names will be a problem when searching for information. Let students brainstorm ways to deal with the problem. (There are charts with both names in some encyclopedias and many books on mythology.)

Where to Research

Use a *Biography Pathfinder Sheet (Appendix)* to help students brainstorm resources.

■ **R**eview the use of print resources, encyclopedias, CD-ROMs, and the Internet. Where else might students look for information on Greek and Roman mythology? As students suggest sources, explore how information is to be found in said resources. For example: How do you locate information within a Web site? (Discuss menus, search options, the find option of the browser, etc.) If you do not find information in a volume of the encyclopedia, what is the next step? (Try the index.)

As Students Work

◆ Assist students as they are locating information. Provide feedback as students summarize their stories. Watch for copying sources word-for-word and help individual students make the transition to taking notes. Remind students to look in multiple resources and to credit their sources on the *Source Credit Sheet*.

- If students download pictures of their characters off the Internet, they will need to record the source of the image on an *Image Source Sheet*. If students need to save images to disks, remember to label each disk and keep a record of students' names and corresponding file names.

- Talk with students about the concept of summarizing.

Compiling the Project

- Direct students to finish their summaries first, then work on the sketches. Encourage neat handwriting.

- Sketches should be labeled with the character's name and title.

Self-Check

Once their projects are nearing completion, refer students to the *Gods, Goddesses, and Ancient Heroes Self-Check Sheet* you handed to them at the beginning of the lesson. Have them assess their own work, or trade with a partner for gentle critique. Then, give students time to polish their projects.

Sharing With the Class

- Ask students to share their myths and their sketches with the class. Choose whether you would prefer students to read their summaries or to tell their myths as stories. The Appendix contains a *Storytelling Tips Sheet* for presenters and a *Presentation Notes Sheet* on which listeners can record feedback.

- Use the *Who's Who of the Gods and Goddesses Sheet* for students to fill out as they are listening to the presentations. (Note: Not all of the characters are listed on the sheet.)

- Another way to use the *Who's Who of the Gods and Goddesses Sheet* is to send students on a scavenger hunt to fill in the form after the sketches are posted.

It's All Greek

After the presentations, students have enough information to complete *It is All Greek Word Connections Sheet* and *Who Will Buy a Piece of the Past? Sheet*. Allow students to break into pairs, and give them twenty minutes to complete the sheets. Then review them as a class.

Adaptations and Extensions

- **I**nvite students to use the frames on their *Greek and Roman Mythology Notetaking Sheets* just for rough sketches. Have them do a larger portrait or have the whole class do a mural of the mythological beings.

- **H**ave students use what they have learned about mythological personalities to write a newspaper with headline stories, obituaries, recipes, police reports, comics, advice columns, and more.

- **U**se the *It's a Myth!* Sheet to do a similar project with the mythologies of other cultures. Compare the similarities and differences.

- **A**s a class, create a mythology family tree. Create with pen and paper or use appropriate software like Inspiration.

- **L**ink this project to studying astronomy.

- **C**ombine this project with a study of mythology and modern language. Use the *It is All Greek Word Connections Sheet* to prompt students to think about the connections between words with mythological origins and the original stories and meanings.

- **G**reek and Roman mythology is part of everyday life. Use the *Who Will Buy a Piece of the Past?* Sheet to introduce a unit on propaganda. Have students design sales campaigns using mythological characters.

- **V**isit the *Project Idea List* in the *Appendix* of this book for additional extension ideas.

Gods, Goddesses, and Ancient Heroes Notetaking Sheet

Name ____

Character's Name:

Greek ________________________________   Roman ______________________________

God/Goddess of (if applicable): ________________________________

Relatives (if any):

Mother: ________________________________   Father: ______________________________

Others: ____

____

Summarize a story about your character: ____

____

____

____

____

____

____

____

____

____

______________________________   Draw a picture of your mythological being.

Name _______________________________

Who's Who of the Gods and Goddesses

	Greek name	Roman name	God or Goddess of . . .
1.	Aphrodite	Venus	
2.	Apollo	Apollo	
3.	Ares	Mars	
4.	Artemis	Diana	
5.	Athena	Minerva	
6.	Demeter	Ceres	
7.	Dionysus	Bacchus	
8.	Eros	Cupid	
9.	Hades	Pluto	
10.	Hephaestus	Vulcan	
11.	Hera	Juno	
12.	Hermes	Mercury	
13.	Hestia	Vesta	
14.	Persephone	Proserpina	
15.	Poseidon	Neptune	
16.	Zeus	Jupiter	

It's a Myth!

Name _______________________________

Similarities	Differences

It is All Greek Word Connections Sheet

Name _______________________________

Connect the Ancient Greek & English words. Use a dictionary to tell what the English word means. Find out about the story of the Ancient Greek being and then tell how the two are connected.

1. Achilles tendon ▶ ◀ Achilles (hero) _______________________________

____

2. atlas ▶ ◀ Atlas (Titan) _______________________________

____

3. cereal ▶ ◀ Ceres (goddess) _______________________________

____

4. mercury ▶ ◀ Mercury (god) _______________________________

____

5. morphine ▶ ◀ Morpheus (god) _______________________________

____

6. pandemonium ▶ ◀ Pandora (mortal) _______________________________

____

7. siren ▶ ◀ Sirens (creatures) _______________________________

____

8. volcano ▶ ◀ Vulcan (god) _______________________________

____

Name ______________________________

Who Will Buy a Piece of the Past?

Did you know that you may be buying a bit of the past when you go shopping? Many business names have roots in Ancient Grecian and Roman mythology. Here is your chance to figure out why certain kinds of businesses have used mythology for their names.

	Business	Mythology	Why is this a good name for the product/company
1.	**Amazon**.com- online bookstore	tribe of warrior women	
2.	**Aries**- car model	God of War	
3.	**Atlas** Van Lines- moving company	a Titan who had to carry the world on his shoulders	
4.	**Hermes**- FTD flower delivery symbol	Messenger God with winged feet	
5.	**Mars**- candy bar	God of War	
6.	**Mercury**- record label, car model	Messenger God with winged feet	
7.	**Midas**- brake and muffler company	king with the golden touch	
8.	**Nike**- running shoes	Goddess of Victory with wings	
9.	**Orion**- company that makes movies	Artemis killed a great hunter and made him into a constellation	
10.	**Poseidon** seafood product brand	God of the Sea	
11.	**Saturn**- automobile company	God of Agriculture Father of Zeus	

Reproducible

Gods, Goddesses, and Ancient Heroes Sign-Up Sheet

Persona	Student Name		Persona	Student Name
Achilles			Andromeda	
Aphrodite			Apollo	
Ares			Artemis	
Atlanta			Athena	
Atlas			Bellerophon	
Cronus			Daedalus	
Demeter			Dionysus	
Echo			Eros	
Gaea			Hades	
Helios			Hephaestus	
Hera			Hercules	
Hermes			Hestia	
Icarus			Jason	
Medusa			Narcissus	
Orpheus			Pandora	
Perseus			Persephone	
Phaethon			Poseidon	
Prometheus			Psyche	
Rhea			Theseus	
Uranus			Zeus	

Reproducible

Name _______________________________________

Title/Project _______________________________

Check the word in each section that best describes your project.

	Not yet! ☹	Sometimes	Often	Yes! ☺
My project is full of information which is accurate, clear, complete, and detailed. I did not copy.				
My writing is neat, easy to read, and makes sense. I have great details.				
My punctuation, spelling, capitals, and grammar are correct.				
I labeled my work to help people understand my project. My label tells the name of the character. If they are a god or goddess, the labels tell of what they are god or goddess.				
I followed directions.				
Art Project: I used lots of color, and was neat and careful when I worked. My project is unique.				
Presentation Project: I was loud and easy to hear. I used visual aids well.				

Comments on back:

Name ________________________ Date ____/____/____ Title/Project ________________________

Gods, Goddesses, & Ancient Heroes Biography Project Rubric

	Apprentice ☹	Journeyman	Master ☺		
	1	2	3	4	
Information: inaccurate, unclear, incomplete, lacking details, credit is not given when appropriate, evidence of copying					Accurate, clear, complete, detailed, sources credited, original work
Mechanics: sloppy, poor spelling, missing capitalization and/or punctuation, poor grammar, difficult to read, illogical, unorganized					Neat, careful, accurate spelling, correct capitalization and punctuation, good grammar, easy to read, logical, organized
Labels or Explanations: no labels, labels incomplete					Labels are complete.
Project Basics: lacking details, does not communicate information, did not follow directions					Good details, communicates information, followed directions
Art Project: lacks color, not original, sloppy					Colorful, original, careful, neat
Presentation Project: hard to hear, poor planning, no or poor use of visuals					Loud and clear, well planned, used visual aids well
	1	2	3	4	
	Apprentice ☹	Journeyman	Master ☺		

Comments on back:

Unit Four

Presenting Poets

Overview

Using the *Presenting Poets Notetaking Sheet,* students will select a poet to research and locate poems that interest them. Each student will create a personal illustrated anthology on a theme using the *Presenting Poets Project Information Sheet* and *Presenting Poets Anthology Planning & Check Sheet.* The anthology will include at least four or five illustrated poems and
a biography of their selected poet. At least two of the poems must be by their "featured" poet. Anthologies can be word-processed or handwritten, and bound with staples or other bookbinding method. Finally, students use the *Presenting Poets Self-Check Sheet* to review their project. Students will share a poem during a Class Coffee House. Use the *Presenting Poets Rubric* to grade each project.

Time Required

Instruction and Research: Three class periods.

Compiling the Projects: For written anthologies, allow two class periods. Time for word processing will depend on availability of computers per student. Recruit parent volunteers for typing if time is short.

Presentations: Two class periods.

Curriculum Connections

Technology, art, literature, reading, writing, and speaking.

Prerequisite Skills

Students should have some familiarity with poets and poetry. If students need this information, introduce it the day before. If the anthologies will be word-processed, students need keyboarding skills. Work with the librarian/media specialist to make sure that students have the needed Dewey, book attack, topic, and electronic search strategies and skills.

MATERIALS

All reproducibles for this lesson are available at the end of the unit except the *Biography Pathfinder Sheet, Source Credit Sheet,* and *Image Credit Sheet,* which are in the Appendix.

Students: *Presenting Poets Notetaking Sheet, Presenting Poets Project Information Sheet, Presenting Poets Anthology Planning and Check Sheet, Biography Pathfinder Sheet, Source Credit Sheet, Image Credit Sheet* (if students download images for their projects), *Presenting Poets Self-Check Sheet, What makes a Good Reader? Sheet,* poetry books, informational books, Internet access, computer workstations with color printers, computer disks, scanner, multimedia projector (if available), art supplies (if illustrations are original), and paper.

Teacher: *Presenting Poet Rubric* for each student, and *Presenting Poets Biography Sign-Up Sheet.*

Coffee House: a camera, beverages (e.g. lemonade or iced tea), cookies, cups, and napkins.

Prepare Your Students

Begin by sharing a personal collection of favorite poems. An expressive reading of fun and outrageous poems is a good way to get students' attention. Tell students that they are going to get to put together their own collection, or anthology, of poems.

Explain what an anthology is. Share examples of anthologies (poetry, short story, etc.) and look at the parts:

- title page
- table of contents
- bibliography
- author
- title
- subject indexes

Discuss with students the idea of theme. Look at the themes of several anthologies. Explain that their anthologies will be based around a theme and featuring a poet.

Distribute *Presenting Poets Anthology Project Information Sheet*. Tell students four or five poems must be included in the anthologies, and that two poems must be by the featured poet. Review the required components:

- theme
- author biography
- title page
- table of contents
- bibliography
- author, title, and subject indexes

Show examples from past years if available.

Poetry Anthology Suggestions

All the Small Poems and Fourteen More—Valerie Worth

Fresh Paint—Eve Merriam

One at a Time—David McCord

Where the Sidewalk Ends—Shel Silverstein

The Random House Book of Poetry for Children—Prelutsky and Lobel

Introducing the Lesson

Distribute and review the *Presenting Poets Notetaking Sheet*, discussing the needed information. (See discussion on *Notetaking Sheets* in How to Use This Book.)

- **P**oint out that not all poets are alike (i.e. some poets may be dead and other are still alive) and that only the appropriate parts of the form should be completed.

- **D**iscuss why some things have to be copied exactly (addresses, recipes, and poems). Talk about the difference between copying a fact like a phone number and a creative work like a poem. Let students know that part of the reason it is acceptable to use a poem in their collection is that they are students and that they are only quoting one small part of a book. They are also giving the author credit. Require students to fill out a *Source Credit Sheet* for all research and poetry sources.

- **A**llow students to select a poet from the *Presenting Poets Biography Sign-Up Sheet*. Students can choose other poets if they like, however, not every poet is researchable. Consider limiting the number of individuals researching each poet.

- **F**ill out the *Presenting Poets Biography Sign-Up Sheet*. (Note: If students are not familiar with poetry, allow them to peruse poetry resources before selecting a poet.)

- **D**irect students to choose a theme for their anthologies. Students might create anthologies of poems that are about animals, friends, family, humor, love, school, etc.

Where To Research

- **D**istribute *Biography Pathfinder Sheet*. Discuss the location of poetry resources in the library.

- **L**et students suggest possible resources. When biographies are mentioned, highlight biographical dictionaries and specialized author reference books, Internet sites, and online databases.

- **A**sk students if this is a good project for reading a whole book about a person or if quick information will work.

- **H**ave students discuss why some authors like Robert Browning would be in the encyclopedia and others would not be included.

- **R**emind students that book jackets can be sources for biographical information.

As Students Work

- **D**istribute and review *Presenting Poets Planning and Check Sheet*. Suggest that students keep in mind their themes and number of poems they need as they research.

- **S**tudents start by looking at poetry collections to identify poems and poets that they like.

- **I**f they have not already done so, direct students to select poets.

- **S**tudents may need help locating multiple poems on a theme. Encourage students to select broad themes and if poetry indexes are available, demonstrate how to use them. If students do not have word-processing skills, ask parent volunteers to help with or do word processing. Let students insert clipart or scanned artwork.

- **A**ssist students as they research. Watch for copying sources word-for-word and help individual students make the transition to taking notes. Remind students to look in multiple resources and to credit their sources on the *Source Credit Sheet*.

- **I**f students download pictures off the Internet, they will need to record the source of the image on an *Image Source Sheet*. If students need to save images to disks, remember to label each disk and keep a record of students' names and corresponding file names.

Compiling the Project

- **D**irect students to refer to the *Presenting Poets Anthology Project Information Sheet* as they put their anthologies together. If they are not typing, encourage neat handwriting.

- **B**efore students begin word processing the anthologies, demonstrate how to center text, change text size and style, add page numbers, and insert page breaks. A multimedia projector works well for demonstrations. Show students how to locate and insert clipart.

- **I**f desired, scan and print original artwork for poem illustration.

Self-Check

Once their projects are nearing completion, distribute *Presenting Poets Self-Check Sheet*. Let students assess their own work, or trade with a partner for gentle critique. Then, give students time to polish their projects.

Sharing With the Class

Prepare students to share poems:

- **E**ncourage them to select a poem from their anthologies that they like.

- **D**istribute and discuss *What Makes a Good Reader? Sheet*.

- **C**onsider allowing students to practice reading aloud in small groups before inviting guests to your Class Coffee House. Let students use the *Presentation Notes Sheet* (Appendix) to provide feedback.

- **T**o discourage fidgeting listeners, serve refreshments before the reading begins or during an intermission.

Adaptations and Extensions

- **M**ake the book a combination art and English project. Ask the art teacher to work with students on bookbinding or challenge students with creating more sophisticated books.

- **H**ave a student committee create invitations and a program for the Class Coffee House.

- **C**hallenge advanced students by having them research the coffee houses and the Beat Generation and share their findings as part of the Class Coffee House.

- **S**tudents can make illustrated poem posters featuring individual poems.

- **U**se fabric markers to create a Poetry Crazy Quilt. Each student writes a poem on a square (original or a favorite by a credited poet) and the squares are sewn together. The favorite poem squares can have the line, "selected by __________" to record each student's name.

- **H**ave each student bring in a gift bag with his/her name written in the bag. Over the school year when students find poems and other writings that they like, copies can be made (with bibliographic information), and the copy can be placed in the bags.

- **V**isit the *Project Idea List* in the *Appendix* of this book for additional extension ideas.

Reproducible

Presenting Poets Notetaking Sheet

Name _______________________________

Poet's Name _______________________________

Date of birth: _________________   Date of death: _________________

Place of birth: _________________

Background information:

Father: _____________________________   Mother: _____________________________

Siblings (brothers & sisters): _____________________________

____

Spouse (husband or wife—if married): _____________________________

Children: _____________________________

____

Education (if any): _____________________________

____

Place(s) lived: _____________________________

____

Jobs: _____________________________

____

____

Attach another sheet as needed.

Presenting Poets Notetaking Sheet

Personal stories (childhood, family, adult life, etc.): ________________________

____

____

____

____

____

Did this poet have any special writing training? ________

What kind of training did he/she have? ________________________________

____

What type of works besides poetry (children's, poetry, plays, nonfiction, mysteries, etc.) does this poet write?

____

____

List some of the poet's famous works: ________________________________

____

____

____

____

Attach another sheet as needed.

Presenting Poets Notetaking Sheet

Why is this poet famous? What makes his/her writing special? _______________

____

____

____

____

What awards, if any, has this poet won? ______________________________

____

____

____

____

Interesting facts about the poet: _________________________________

____

____

____

____

____

____

____

Attach another sheet as needed.

Reproducible

Presenting Poets Anthology Planning & Check Sheet

Name ________________________________

Poet's Name ________________________________

Anthology theme: ________________________________

Title of anthology:________________________________

Check when you have the item completed:

Title page _______

Table of Contents _______

Four or Five Poems _______

Two Poems by featured poet _______

Poet biography _______

Bibliography _______

Index _______

Reproducible

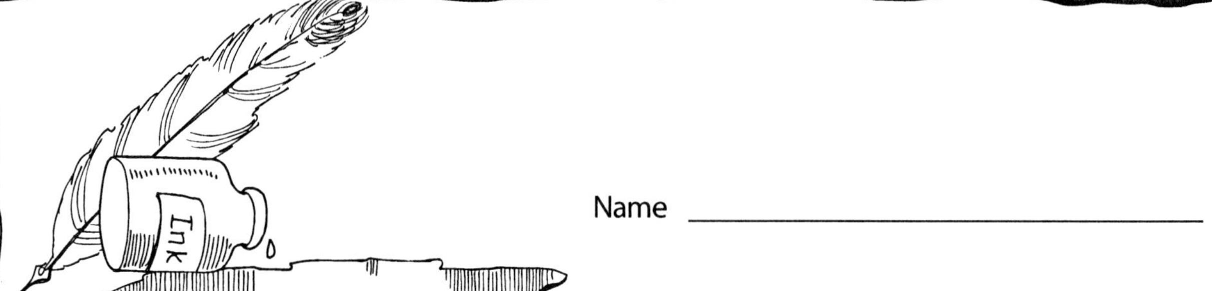

Presenting Poets Project Information Sheet

Name _______________________________

Your project is to make an illustrated poetry anthology. Your anthology will have a theme and feature at least two poems by one author and a biography of that poet.

Things to think about:

What theme do you want your book to have? Do you have any favorite poets? What kinds of poems do they write? Does your poet have any special types of theme that they use when they write?

- ◆ Who will be listening to the poems you select and reading your anthology?
- ◆ Should that make any difference when you are selecting your themes and poems?

What type of **artwork** will work illustrate the poems?

- ◆ color, black & white, paint (spatter or finger), water color, stickers, acrylics, mosaics, pencils, color pencils, markers, cut pieces of fabric, yarn, ribbon, prints, computer graphics, collage (pictures or other items), cut pieces of paper, photographs, etc.

How will the **lettering** be done?

- ◆ hand written (cursive or print), typed, or computer print-out

How will you **bind** the book?

- ◆ staples, brass fasteners, accordion fold, rings, laces, notebook fasteners, spiral binding, hand or machine stitched, report covers, etc.

What **materials** will you use?

- ◆ paper, construction paper, cardboard, contact paper, poster board, wall paper, gift wrap, fabric, foil, etc.

Presenting Poets Project Information Sheet

The process:

1. Search for **poems** and research the **poet**.

    Think about what kind(s) of illustrations would be best for your book.

2. **Write** the poet's biography.

3. **Organize** the book.

    Decide and design how your book pages will look and work.

    Decide what words will be on which page. Sketch pictures on the pages with the words. This is called the **layout** of the book.

4. Make a **dummy** (rough draft of your book).

    Include a:

title page	copyright page	dedication page
Dog Poems Collected by Kay Norris MGHS Publishing, Inc. Mount Gilead, Ohio	 MGHS Publishing, Inc. Mount Gilead, Ohio	 This book is dedicated to Carson, Belle, & Sandy

Reproducible

5. **Edit** your rough draft. (Make corrections and improvements to your story.)

   Have people read it and make suggestions.

   Are things written and spelled correctly?

   Do the pictures make sense and do they help to illustrate the poems?

6. **Create** your book.

   artwork

   binding

7. **Share** the poems and your book with classmates.

Reproducible

Presenting Poets Biography Sign-Up Sheet

Poet	Student Name		Poet	Student Name
Maya Angelou			William Blake	
Robert Browning			Lewis Carroll	
John Ciardi			e.e. cummings	
Walter De La Mare			Beatrice Schenk de Regniers	
T.S. Eliot			Eleanor Farjeon	
Paul Fleishman			Robert Frost	
Florence Parry Heide			Mary Ann Hoberman	
Langston Hughes			K.J. Kennedy	
Edward Lear			Myra Cohn Livingston	
Henry Wadsworth Longfellow			Eve Merriam	
A.A. Milne			Ogden Nash	
Jack Prelutsky			Carl Sandburg	
Shel Silverstein			Robert Louis Stevenson	
Walter Tripp			Judith Viorst	
Nancy Willard			Jan Yolen	

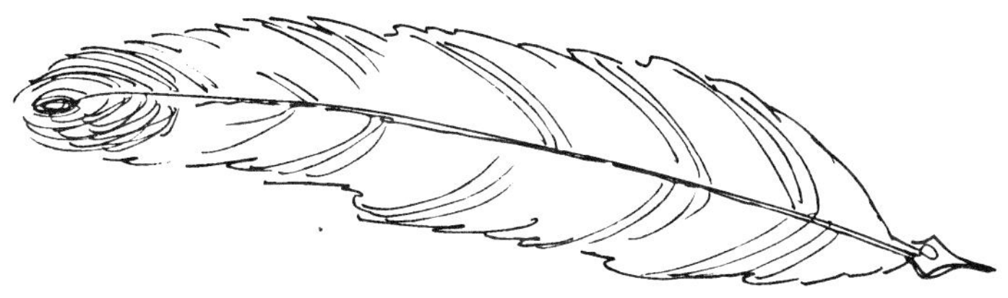

What Makes a Good Reader?

- "Hey, look me over." Do you look neat and clean?

- Have pauses. Take time to breath. Give your listeners time to think about what you are reading.

- Avoid reading too fast. People will not be able to understand you.

- Read with expression. Think of how the person who is most likely to put you asleep talks. Now think of the most exciting speaker you know.

- Practice.

- What do you think; is chewing gum a good idea?

- Avoid wild gestures or rocking back and forth. While you want your poem to be interesting you do not want people to watch what you are doing instead of listening to the poem.

- Project your voice. Talk to the back of the room. You can whisper and be heard in a huge room if you know how. Practice! Make sure you are not mumbling.

- Think good eye contact. Look at as many people as possible. If that is too uncomfortable look just over the tops of peoples' heads.

- Pick a friendly face. Find someone who is smiling and look at him or her.

- Give credit! Tell where you got the poem. Who is the author?

Presenting Poets Self-Check Sheet

Name _______________________________

Title/Project _______________________________

Check the word in each section that best describes your project.

	Not yet! ☹	Sometimes	Often	Yes! ☺
My project is full of information which is accurate, clear, complete, realistic, and detailed. I did not copy information about my poet and gave credit for the information I used.				
My writing is neat and easy to read.				
My punctuation, spelling, capitals, and grammar are correct.				
My writing makes sense.				
My illustrations are colorful, neat, and unique.				
My illustrations match the poems.				
I planned my project and followed directions. My book has a cover, title page, table of contents, and an index. It includes the required number of poems and a biographical entry on my poet.				
I was loud and easy to hear. I read with expression and used visual aids well.				

Comments on back:

Name _______________ Date ___/___/___ Title/Project _______________

Presenting Poets Rubric

| | Apprentice | Journeyman | | Master | |
	😟 1	2	3	😊 4	
Information: inaccurate, unclear, incomplete, lacking details, credit is not given when appropriate, evidence of copying					Accurate, clear, complete, detailed, sources credited, original work
Mechanics: sloppy, poor spelling, missing capitalization and/or punctuation, poor grammar, difficult to read, illogical, unorganized					Neat, careful, accurate spelling, correct capitalization and punctuation, good grammar, easy to read, logical, organized
Labels or Explanations: no labels or explanations					Labels or explanations help the "audience" to better understand the information presented
Project Basics: I did not follow directions; missing poet biography, cover, title, page, table of contents, and/or index; too few poems.					Follows directions; includes poet biography, cover, title, page, table of contents, index, and required number of poems
Illustrations: lacks color, not original, sloppy, do not match poems					Colorful, original, careful, neat, match poems
Presentation Project: hard to hear, no or poor use of visuals, no expression					Loud and clear, read with expression, used visual aids well
	😟 1	2	3	😊 4	
	Apprentice	Journeyman		Master	

Comments on back:

Unit Five

Super Students

Overview

Using the *Super Student Notetaking Sheet* and *Friend or Family Interview Sheet*, students will research information about their own lives, and then write and illustrate autobiographies. Using the *Editor's Marks Sheet* students will break into editorial conferences to review their peers' projects. The autobiographies will be "published" in a class collective biography for the class library. Individual chapters can be printed out and sent home with students, and students can check out the collective biography to take home. Students use *Autobiography Self-Check Sheet* for a final review of their autobiographies. Finally, use the *Autobiography Rubric* to grade each project.

Time Required

Instruction and Research: One to two class periods, depending on how much information students can gather from home.

Compiling the Projects: Two class periods for writing and one class period for editorial conferences and re-writes. If entries are to be word processed by students, additional time needed will depend on student skill level and availability of computers. Recruit parent volunteers for typing if time is short.

Curriculum Connections

Technology, art, reading, and writing.

Prerequisite Skills

Word processing skills (optional).

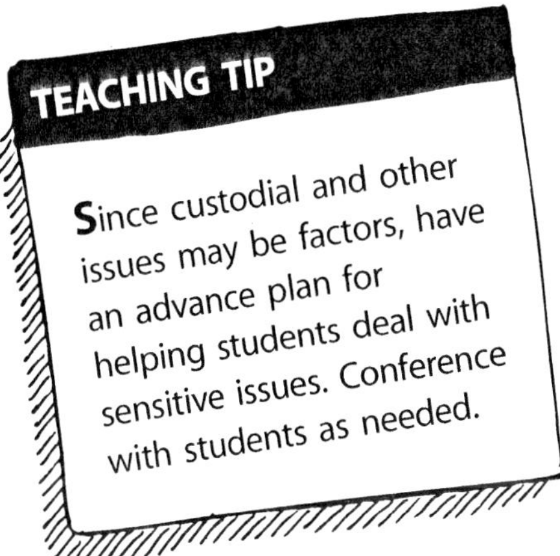

BIOGRAPHY RESOURCES

American Biography—
Eric Lundman

Black Authors and Illustrators of Children's Books—
Garland

Preparing Your Students

Start the lesson by sharing a funny personal story about grade school days. Then ask students if there are surprising or funny stories about themselves that would be fun to share with the class. Tell them that they are all going to have a chance to share because the class is going to create a book of biographies featuring the members of the class.

Optional: Show examples of collective biographies. Compare and contrast the biographical dictionary entry, a biography in a collective biography and a complete traditional biography/autobiography.

Show class collective biography projects from past years, if available.

Introducing the Lesson

- ◆ Distribute and review *Super Student Notetaking Sheet*. Discuss examples of information that could be used to fill in blanks. Ask if there are some additional types of information or questions that should be added to the back of their *Notetaking Sheets*.

- ◆ Discuss the idea of personal versus public information with students. Help them understand that some things are too personal to share in a class/public publication.

- ◆ Send a letter home explaining the project to parents/guardians. (See page 88.)

Where to Research

- ■ **R**efer to the *Primary and Secondary Source* mini-lesson in Unit One. As a class, brainstorm examples of primary and secondary sources. Star the ones that the class feels are likely to be most useful.

- ■ **D**irect students to create a personal list of primary and secondary sources about their lives. Suggest they list as possible interview candidates any people who know good stories about them.

- ■ **D**istribute and review *Friend or Family Interview Sheet*. Require students to interview at least one friend or family member. Discuss:

  - ◆ developing and writing down questions in advance,

  - ◆ scheduling an interview,

  - ◆ and recording responses.

  Encourage students to follow-up the interview with a thank-you note. Consider making the thank-you note a requirement.

As Students Work

■ **I**f you created a topic outline for the class to follow, remind them of that before they begin their drafts.

■ **R**emind students to incorporate information they received from their interviews into their autobiographies.

■ **A**s the editor of the class biography, have prepublication conferences with students about their drafts. Give students a copy of the *Editor's Marks Sheet*. (Note: There are four copies of editing marks per sheet.)

Compiling the Project

◆ Show students how to scan photographs and save files. If a digital camera is available, have students take current photographs of each other.

◆ Demonstrate how to locate and insert picture files. A multimedia projector works well for demonstrations.

◆ Students may also bring photos of themselves to paste onto their autobiographies, or they may draw pictures of themselves.

◆ After the documents are written or typed, let students break into groups for editorial conferences. Students should use their *Editor's Marks Sheets* to mark needed corrections.

◆ The first students to complete their autobiographies can be charged with creating a cover, title page, and table of contents.

Self-Check

Once their autobiographies are nearing completion, distribute
Autobiography Self-Check Sheet for a final project review. Let
students assess their own work, or trade with a partner for gentle
critique. Then, give students time to polish their projects.

Sharing With the Class

Insert the collective biography into a three ring binder, or use any
bookbinding technique you learned in Unit Four to bind your
class collective biography. Allow students to check out and take
the class collective biography home.

Adaptations and Extensions

- Create a class map showing the student birth places.

- Make creating a class scrapbook a yearlong project.

- Have students summarize their autobiographies as news
  articles in a class or the school newspaper.

- Chart and compare information (hobbies, foods, sports,
  etc.) from the *Notetaking Sheets*.

- Visit the *Project Idea List* in the *Appendix* of this book for
  additional extension ideas.

Super Students Notetaking Sheet

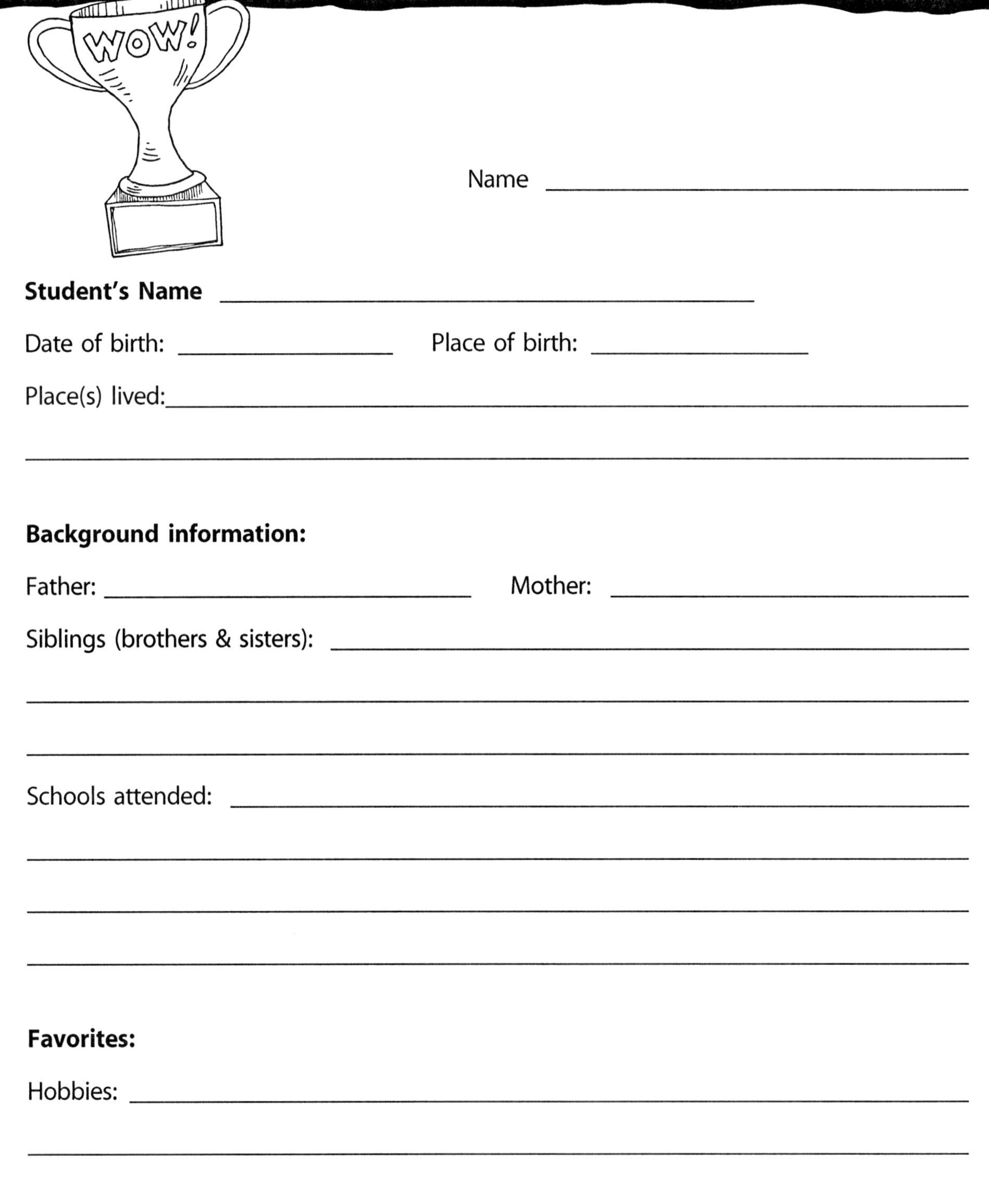

Name _______________________________

Student's Name _______________________________

Date of birth: _______________ Place of birth: _______________

Place(s) lived:_______________________________

____

Background information:

Father: _______________ Mother: _______________

Siblings (brothers & sisters): _______________

____

____

Schools attended: _______________

____

____

____

Favorites:

Hobbies: _______________

____

____

Super Students Notetaking Sheet

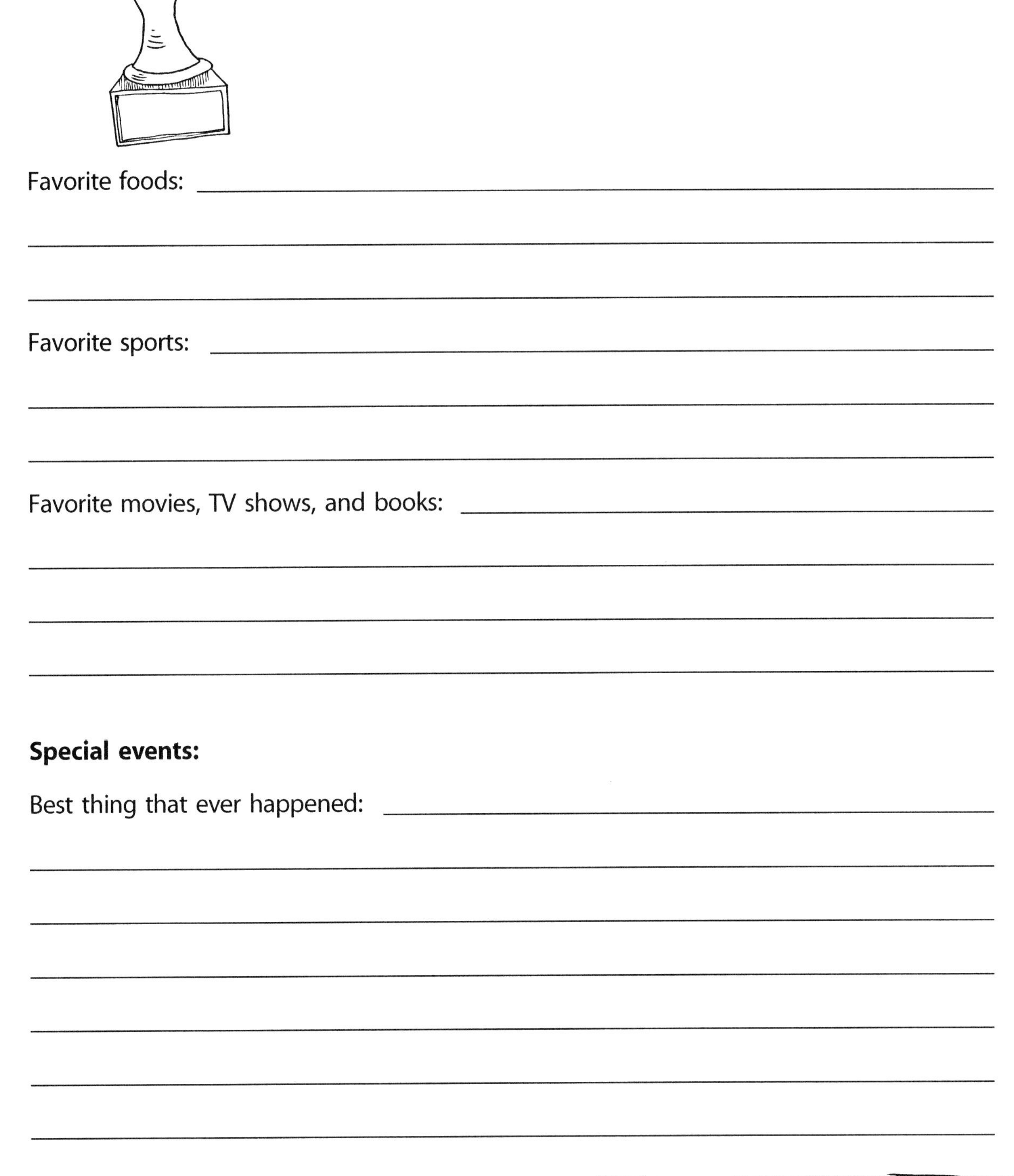

Favorite foods: ____

____

____

Favorite sports: ____

____

____

Favorite movies, TV shows, and books: ________________________

____

____

____

Special events:

Best thing that ever happened: ________________________________

____

____

____

____

____

____

____

Super Students Notetaking Sheet

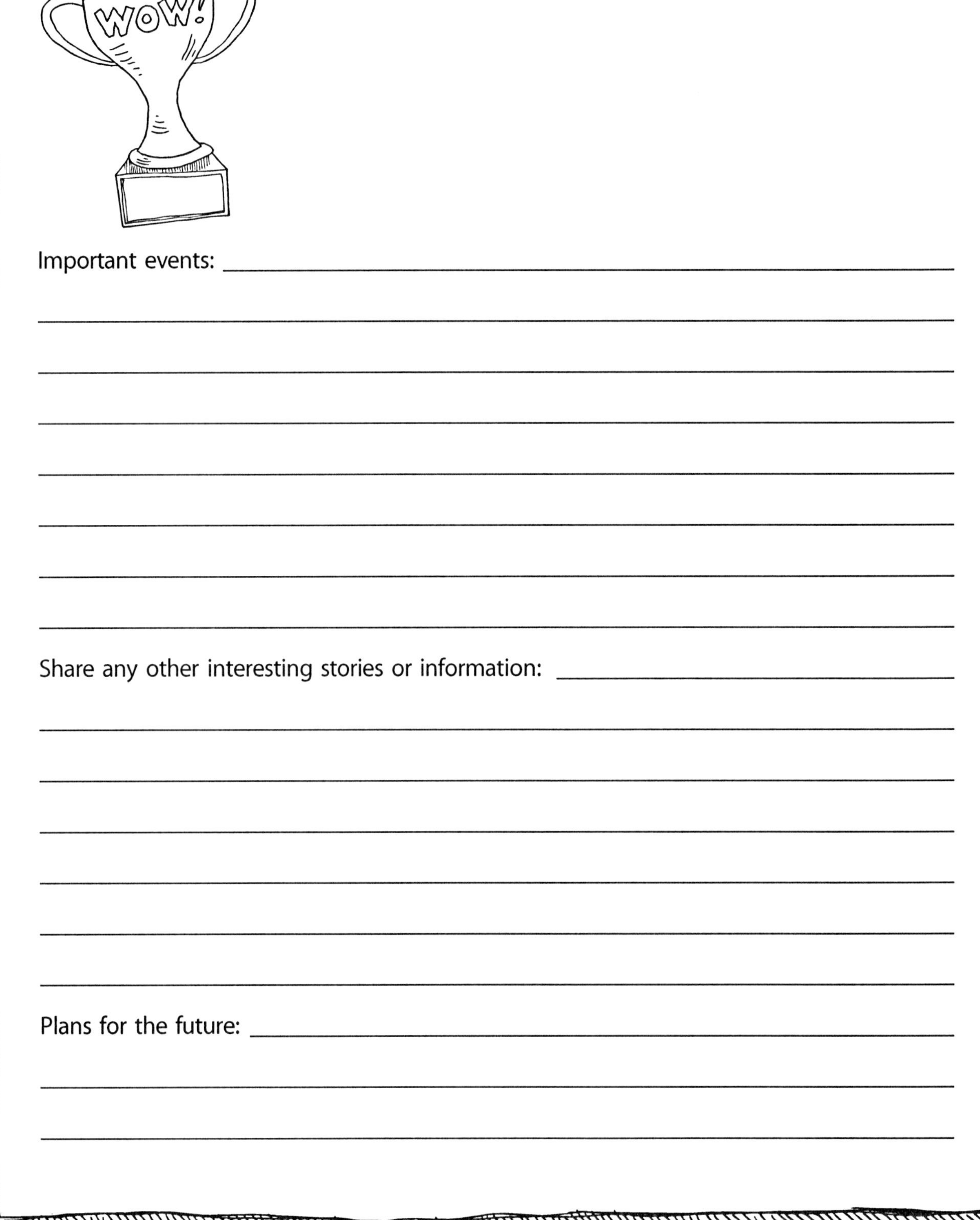

Important events: ____

____

____

____

____

____

____

____

Share any other interesting stories or information: ________________________

____

____

____

____

____

____

Plans for the future: ____

____

____

Friend or Family Interview Sheet

Name ________________________________ Relationship ________________________

Interview date ______________ time _________ place ________________________

Question: ____

____

Answer: ____

____

Question: ____

____

Answer: ____

____

Question: ____

____

Answer: ____

____

Question: ____

____

Answer: ____

____

Send a thank you! ☐ **Comments/Reactions/Ideas to Pursue:** __________

Parent Letter

____

Dear Parent or Guardian,

Our class is creating a collection of class biographies. Your child will be writing his/her own story. As part of the assignment, your child will be interviewing one or more family members or friends.

Your child should also be asking to look at information and records relating to his/her life. Helpful items might include his/her birth certificate, grade cards, letters, award certificates, photographs, and videotapes. Students will be told not to bring items like birth certificates to school. They should ask permission to bring items like photographs to school to be scanned.

If you have any questions or are willing to help with typing, please contact me at _______________________________.

Sincerely,

____

Reproducible

Student Resource Page

Day by Day Information

Biography.com
http://www.biography.com/
Look for the Born on This Day search box.

CNN.com Daily Almanac
http://www.cnn.com/almanac/daily/

The History Channel: This Day in History
http://www.historychannel.com/tdih/
index.html

The History Net: Today in History
http://www.historynet.com/tih/

Infoplease.com: This Day in History
http://www.infoplease.com/cgi-
bin/dayinhistory

Library of Congress: Today in History
http://lcweb2.loc.gov/ammcm/today/
today.html

New York Times: On This Day
http://www.nytimes.com/learning/general/
onthisday/index.html

PBS—On This Day in History
http://www.pbs.org/neighborhoods/history/
daily/1-Jan.html

Yahooligans: This Day in History
http://www.yahooligans.com/docs/tdih/

Year by Year Information:

Decades History Timeline
http://www.decades.com/

History Central.com—The Major Events in World History
http://www.multied.com/dates/Index.html

History Timeline.com
http://www.historytimeline.com/Norm/
normindex.htm

HyperHistory.com—World History
http://www.hyperhistory.com/online_n2/
History_n2/a.html

Infoplease.com: 20th Century Year by Year (covers through the present)
http://www.infoplease.com/millennium1.
html

Reproducible

	Editor's Marks Sheet
sp	Spelling
ro	Run on
frag	Sentence fragment
e	Delete
~	Reverse words or letters
¶	Start a new paragraph
#	Insert a space
∧	Insert a word or letter
∧	Insert comma
∨	Insert quotation marks
ital	Use italics
⊙	Add a period
/	Lowercase letter
=	Capitalize letter
⌣	Close a space
stet	Ignore the correction

	Editor's Marks Sheet
sp	Spelling
ro	Run on
frag	Sentence fragment
e	Delete
~	Reverse words or letters
¶	Start a new paragraph
#	Insert a space
∧	Insert a word or letter
∧	Insert comma
∨	Insert quotation marks
ital	Use italics
⊙	Add a period
/	Lowercase letter
=	Capitalize letter
⌣	Close a space
stet	Ignore the correction

	Editor's Marks Sheet
sp	Spelling
ro	Run on
frag	Sentence fragment
e	Delete
~	Reverse words or letters
¶	Start a new paragraph
#	Insert a space
∧	Insert a word or letter
∧	Insert comma
∨	Insert quotation marks
ital	Use italics
⊙	Add a period
/	Lowercase letter
=	Capitalize letter
⌣	Close a space
stet	Ignore the correction

	Editor's Marks Sheet
sp	Spelling
ro	Run on
frag	Sentence fragment
e	Delete
~	Reverse words or letters
¶	Start a new paragraph
#	Insert a space
∧	Insert a word or letter
∧	Insert comma
∨	Insert quotation marks
ital	Use italics
⊙	Add a period
/	Lowercase letter
=	Capitalize letter
⌣	Close a space
stet	Ignore the correction

Super Student Autobiography Project Self-Check Sheet

Name _______________________________

Title/Project _______________________________

Check the word in each section that best describes
your project.

	Not yet! ☹	Sometimes	Often	Yes! ☺
My project is full of information which is accurate, clear, complete, and realistic. It includes great details. My writing makes sense.				
My punctuation, spelling, capitals, and grammar are correct.				
I have photographs and other illustrations that go with my autobiography. They all have labels.				
I planned my project and followed directions. I conducted at least one interview.				

Comments on back:

Name _______________________ Date _____ / _____ / _____ Title/Project _______________________

Super Student Autobiography Project Rubric

	Apprentice ☹	Journeyman	Master ☺		
	1	2	3	4	
Information: inaccurate, unclear, incomplete, lacking details, credit is not given when appropriate, evidence of copying					Accurate, clear, complete, detailed, sources credited, original work
Mechanics: sloppy, poor spelling, missing capitalization and/or punctuation, poor grammar, difficult to read, illogical, unorganized					Neat, careful, accurate spelling, correct capitalization and punctuation, good grammar, easy to read, logical, organized
Labels or Explanations: no labels or explanations					Pictures and illustrations are labeled and help readers to better understand the information presented
Project Basics: did not follow directions & did not do an interview					Followed directions and did at least one interview
Illustrations: no photos or illustrations to go with the text					Appropriate photos and illustrations complement the text
	1	2	3	4	
	Apprentice ☹	Journeyman	Master ☺		

Comments on back:

Appendix

Project Idea List

1. **Advertise the person's innovation with a:**

   radio, TV, newspaper, travel poster, brochure, or poster ad.

2. **Make a:**

   diorama, movie box or peep box showing the person's life and/or accomplishments.

3. **Write a script using information about the topic and perform it.**

   Consider using: video camera, puppets, tape recorder, no words (be a mime) or a flannel board. Put on a TV drama, situation comedy, game show, talk show, campaign speech, etc. featuring the famous person.

4. **Dress up like the person and:**

   tell about "your invention/accomplishment;" life; act out an interview; or have a job interview.

5. **Draw, paint, or create a:**

   computerized slide show, mobile, T-shirt, mural, bulletin board, cartoon strip (animate), comic book, scrapbook/album, life size portrait, paper doll(s), series of pictures, series of photos (photo album), baseball-style card, map showing important places, family tree, or collage about the individual.

6. **Design and make a famous person:**

   model, mask, character doll(s) fabric banner, quilt, set of trading card, word game, or puzzle.

7. **Put together a:**

   collection of objects, time capsule, timeline, calendar, day planner/schedule, or project in a bag, suitcase, Web page, quilt, passport, can, or box telling about the person.

8. **In character write:**

   letters, postcards, greeting cards, an apology, an editorial, a ballad, or a diary

9. **Publish a famous person book with:**

   story based on facts, how-to information, fascinating facts, biography information, poems, songs (possibly raps or cheers), book jacket, or quotations.

10. **Create a famous person:**

    pathfinder, Web page, magazine article, front page newspaper, award, epitaph, life story theatre program, coat of arms, or police report/file.

Biography Pathfinder

First name   Last name

Search sources:

1. Encyclopedias:

    ◆ ____

    ◆ ____

2. Internet search plan:

    ◆ ____

    ◆ ____

3. Online databases to search:

    ◆ ____

    ◆ ____

4. Specialized reference books (biographical dictionaries and other
    biographical resources):

    ◆ ____

    ◆ ____

5. Books via the card catalog (subjects to search):

    ◆ ____

    ◆ ____

6. Other sources (magazines, experts, etc.):

    ◆ ____

    ◆ ____

    ◆ ____

Source Credit Sheet

Name _______________

#	Resource (Book, Encyclopedia, Magazine, Website, CD ROM, etc.)	Title (Book, Encyclopedia and Article, Magazine and Article, etc.)	Author/Editor	URL or Publisher	Place Published	Date	Pages

Name _______________________________

Image Credit Sheet

Title of Web site/print source: _______________________________

Image owner/artist: _______________________________ Date: _______________

Address (URL) of Web site or name of publisher: _______________________________

Name _______________________________

Image Credit Sheet

Title of Web site/print source: _______________________________

Image owner/artist: _______________________________ Date: _______________

Address (URL) of Web site or name of publisher: _______________________________

Name _______________________________

Image Credit Sheet

Title of Web site/print source: _______________________________

Image owner/artist: _______________________________ Date: _______________

Address (URL) of Web site or name of publisher: _______________________________

Name _______________________________

Image Credit Sheet

Title of Web site/print source: _______________________________

Image owner/artist: _______________________________ Date: _______________

Address (URL) of Web site or name of publisher: _______________________________

Reproducible

International Biography Sign-Up Sheet

International	Student Name	International	Student Name
Czar Nicholas II, ruler		Julius Caesar, ruler	
Alexander the Great, ruler		Cleopatra, queen	
Mohandas Gandhi, leader		Mother Theresa, social worker	
Joan of Arc, leader		Queen Elizabeth I, queen	
Florence Nightingale, nurse		Beatrix Potter, writer	
Fidel Castro, dictator		Ludwig Von Beethoven, musician	
Charles Dickens, writer		Joseph Stalin, dictator	
Louis Pasteur, inventor		Pancho Villa, general	
Santa Anna, general		Sir Isaac Newton, scientist	
La Salle, explorer		King Louis XIV, leader	
King Louis XVI, leader		Marie Antoinette, queen	
Marco Polo, explorer		Johannes Gutenberg, inventor	
William Shakespeare, writer		Cortes, explorer	
Queen Victoria, leader		Napoleon Bonaparte, general	
Wolfgang Amadeus Mozart, musician		Louis Braille, inventor	
Aristotle, philosopher			

Reproducible

American Biography Sign-Up Sheet

American	Student Name	American	Student Name
Jane Addams, social worker		Mohammed Ali, athlete	
Louisa Mae Alcott, writer		Susan B. Anthony, women's rights	
Louis Armstrong, musician		Neil Armstrong, astronaut	
Arthur Ashe, athlete		P.T. Barnum, showman	
Daniel Boone, frontiersman		Clara Barton, nurse	
Alexander Graham Bell, inventor		Matthew Brady, photographer	
Sitting Bull, Native American Chief		Andrew Carnegie, businessman	
George Rogers Clark, explorer		Buffalo Bill Cody, westerner	
Davy Crockett, frontiersman		Crazy Horse, Native American	
Bill Cosby, entertainer		George A. Custer, general	
Jefferson Davis, Confederate President		Joe DiMaggio, athlete	
Walt Disney, entertainer		Amelia Earhart, pilot	
Thomas Edison, inventor		Duke Ellington, musician	
Henry Ford, inventor		Benjamin Franklin, statesman	
Bill Gates, buisnessman		Lou Gehrig, athlete	

American Biography Sign-Up Sheet

American	Student Name		American	Student Name
John Glen, astronaut			Ulysses S. Grant, President	
Wild Bill Hickock, frontiersman			J. Edgar Hoover, head of FBI	
Harry Houdini, magician			Sam Houston, frontiersman	
Howard Hughes, inventor			Helen Keller, writer	
Robert E. Lee, general			Charles Lindberg, adventurer	
Joe Louis, athlete			Douglas MacArthur, general	
Mickey Mantle, athlete			Francis Marion, soldier	
Margaret Mead, anthropologist			Marilyn Monroe, entertainer	
Samuel Morse, inventor			Annie Oakley, sharpshooter	
Rosa Parks, civil rights leader			Allan Pinkerton, detective	
Pocahontas, Native American			Edgar Allan Poe, writer	
Elvis Presley, entertainer			Paul Revere, patriot	
Jackie Robinson, athlete			John D. Rockefeller, Vice President	
Will Rogers, entertainer			Eleanor Roosevelt, first lady	
Betsy Ross, patriot			Babe Ruth, athlete	

Reproducible

American Biography Sign-Up Sheet

American	Student Name		American	Student Name
Sacagawea, American Indian			William Tecumseh Sherman, general	
Harriet Beecher Stowe, writer			John Phillip Sousa, musician	
Annie Sullivan, teacher			Tecumseh, Native American	
Shirley Temple, entertainer			Jim Thorpe, athlete	
Harriet Tubman, abolitionist			Mark Twain, writer	
John Wayne, entertainer			Mad Anthony Wayne, soldier	
Laura Ingalls Wilder, writer			Wilbur & Orville Wright, inventors	
Chuck Yeager, record setter				

Biography Sign-Up Sheet 

Person to Research	Student Name		Person to Research	Student Name

*S*torytelling Tips

Pick a story you **LOVE**!

Visualize.

Avoid memorizing.

Keep key words and phrases.

PRACTICE.

Have pauses.

Tell with expression.

Project.

Forget something? "By the way they also..."

Have good eye contact. Pick a friendly face.

SMILE...SMILE...SMILE...SMILE...SMILE...SMILE...SMILE...SMILE...SMILE...

AVOID...

Telling too fast.

Mumbling.

Telling without expression.

Rocking and shuffling.

Wild gestures.

Chewing gum.

"Ya know..., Ur umm..."

Apologizing.

"Thank you."

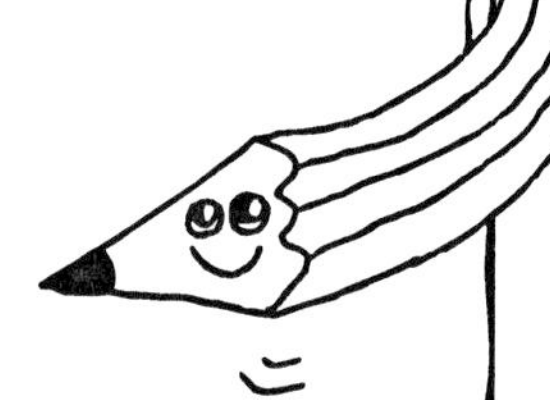

Name ______________________________

Presentation Notes

Presenter's name: ______________________________

I liked the way you ______________________________

____

____

____

____

Next time it would help if you ______________________________

____

____

____

____

I learned ______________________________

____

____

____

____

____

Printed in the United States
1230800001B/2-144